FLY FISHING

100 Things to Know

Fly Fishing

100 Things to Know

Jay Nichols, editor

STACKPOLE
BOOKS

Published by
STACKPOLE BOOKS
5067 Ritter Road
Mechanicsburg, PA 17055
www.stackpolebooks.com

Printed in the United States of America

10 9 8 7 6 5 4 3 2 1

First edition

Cover design by Wendy Reynolds
Cover photo © David Epperson/Photographer's Choice/Getty Images

Library of Congress Cataloging-in-Publication Data

Fly fishing : 100 things to know / Jay Nichols, editor. — 1st ed.
    p. cm.
    ISBN-13: 978-0-8117-3495-0
    ISBN-10: 0-8117-3495-1
    1. Fly fishing. I. Nichols, Jay.
    SH456.F58515 2008

799.12'4—dc22

                                                        2007047991

CONTENTS

Approach and Presentation

Fishing Casts Should Not Be Straight

Unlike the arrow-straight casting-pond casts you see on TV or at fly-fishing shows, most fishing fly casts were developed to introduce slack into the leader, which facilitates a drag-free drift of the fly. The crucial slack isn't always pretty—it may be in the form of a series of S curves or simply a pile of leader on the water's surface—but it gives the fly a few more precious moments to float in a natural fashion before the current attacks the leader and line. And it's surprising how attractive a well-executed slack-line cast begins to look when you know it's the answer to fooling a trout into taking your dry fly.

For a good slack-line cast, make sure your leader is at least 2 feet long, even longer can be better. You'll know if your leader is not long enough if all is straight between your fly line and fly after you cast. If your leader lands in a pile that looks like a bird's nest, you should shorten it up a bit. Ideally, you want a leader with lots of S curves in it.

Drab Colors Blend in with the Surroundings

Professional photographers like a touch of bright color to add life to their fishing pictures or to help an angler stand out in a scenic shot. If you are hoping to make a magazine cover, wear a bright red shirt. If you want to catch trout, leave the red shirt at home and wear something drab. Many good anglers wear camouflage clothing when they fish.

Consider the color of the surroundings of the water you plan to fish and dress accordingly. Many spring creeks are bordered with lush vegetation that presents a green background to the fish. You'll blend into this type of environment best if you wear a green or olive vest, shirt, and hat. Many large western tailwaters are in open country with vast prairie grass and sagebrush meadows. Tan, gray, or khaki clothing might blend in best with these surroundings. In the salt, shirts that are light blue or even white (the color of clouds) blend in well.

A Quiet and Low Approach Works Best

The deception in fly fishing is more than in the fly. You must get close enough to present the fly without being detected. This isn't easy on clear, placid water. No matter how your clothing blends in with the surroundings, you must keep out of the trout's window of vision at all times. On streams where they aren't accustomed to seeing anglers, a trout alerted to your presence will be gone in the blink of an eye. On heavily fished streams, they usually hold their position—they've seen enough blundering anglers to not perceive them as a threat. Either way, a trout that has been alerted will be difficult, if not impossible, to catch.

Use the foliage on the bank to help hide your profile. You can slip along a high bank, or hide beneath a bush or tree and blend into the surroundings. Walking on a high bank with nothing but blue sky behind you is a sure way to convince the trout that it needs to find another place to eat. You can get a little closer to a feeding trout by crouching to keep your profile low. Kneel on one knee so you can get up more quickly. Consider the tip of your fly rod when you are approaching. Keep it behind you so you don't give the trout an early warning of your approach.

Wading Disturbs Fish

When planning your approach, first try to get close enough to cast without wading. Wading creates vibrations, no matter how careful you are, and should be avoided whenever possible. If you do need to wade, avoid grinding the rocks on the bottom. A probing wading staff clinking against rocks or waves on the surface from careless wading signals to fish that trouble lurks nearby. The best way to wade to avoid grinding and wave action is to not shuffle your feet across the bottom. Shuffling also disturbs the bottom and damages the aquatic life. Lift one foot at a time; plant your heel and rock forward to your toe. Murky water can put a fish off its feeding. When you locate a trout and need to position yourself across current from it, try to wade across far enough below it to avoid being detected. If you must wade across from above, try to move far enough upstream so that the clouded water will disappear before it reaches the trout.

Walking on the bank also creates vibrations, which will be easily sensed by a wary trout. Walk softly, carefully, and precisely. Minimizing vibrations is not the only reason to walk slowly and carefully. Nothing terrorizes a trout more than a 200-pound angler doing a half gainer after stepping into a muskrat hole or tripping over a strand of barbed wire.

Wind and Sun Direction Affect Success

Always consider the wind and sun before you get into casting position. There is no reason to handicap yourself by trying to see your fly with the glaring sun in your face or the wind blowing the fly back into your body. If possible, stalk a trout with the sun at your back; you will usually have the advantage of the trout not being able to see you as well. If your shadow suddenly appears to a trout, you can kiss it good bye. It is also easier to see your fly on the water if the sun is at your back. Check the direction of the wind before you try to approach a feeding fish. A stout breeze can dramatically affect your accuracy and distance. If possible, try to get the wind behind you. The worst situation is when the wind blows from your casting arm, across your body.

The First Cast Should Be the Best Cast

The first cast is the most important. Your odds decrease with each additional cast. Most anglers can cast much more accurately at close range, plus the more line on the water, the harder it is to get a drag-free float because there is more surface pulling at the line. The closer you can get to a feeding trout, the better your chances of taking it.

Measure your cast by false casting low and well to the side of the fish before making your presentation cast. Some anglers measure their cast by letting the line flow downstream of them—getting a feel for the amount of line they will need and then verifying that amount with one false cast well to the side of the fish before their presentation cast. To help ensure that you get it right the first time, plan your approach first, and only cast as far as you are comfortable, making sure that you don't have more line out than you need to make the cast—any extra will surely tangle.

False Casts Don't Catch Fish

The best reason to get close is to avoid wasted false casts. Most anglers can cast 20 feet or more without false casting. Even if you are using a dark fly line, you can almost guarantee a spooked trout if you start false casting over him. By minimizing your false casts, you'll also put more casts over the fish instead of in the air.

With weighted flies and lines, false casts are begging for trouble, especially if it is windy. Good anglers have learned to deliver the fly with one (maximum two) false casts—whether in freshwater or saltwater. The best distance casters don't huff and puff and make ten back casts—they get the fly where they want it to go with only one or two false casts. The more you wave the line back and forth, the more chances you have of introducing errors into the cast, wasting precious fishing time, and spooking fish.

Trout Have Distinctive Feeding Rhythms

If you are having a hard time matching the hatch, try matching the trout's feeding rhythm. Some anglers change flies time and again, convinced that their pattern is wrong, when, in fact, they didn't give the trout the chance to see their fly. As the trout starts to rise from its holding position, it drifts downstream with the current. After the trout takes a fly, it goes back upstream to its holding position. If your fly arrives before the trout has reached its holding position and is ready to rise again, it won't be noticed.

Before you make your first cast, wait and watch the trout feed. Often, the more frequently a trout rises, the better your chances to hook it. If there aren't a lot of insects on the water, chances are the trout will take almost all those that drift through its feeding position. The difficulty increases as more insects emerge. The toughest trout are those that let dozens of insects pass by between each rise. Once you get close to the fish and measure your distance, concentrate on timing your casts to match the trout's feeding rhythm. Keep in mind that your odds generally decrease with each successive drift over the fish.

Trout Near the Surface Have Narrow Feeding Lanes

Trout frequently hold close to the surface to inspect their food and expend little energy feeding. Close to the surface, a trout's depth of focus is short and its feeding lane may only be a few inches wide. If you cast your fly outside of this feeding lane, the fish will probably not see it. If a trout is holding 2 or 3 feet under the surface, it has a greater depth of focus and wider feeding lane.

If the fish is feeding and focusing on flies on the surface, it will be unlikely to focus on you unless alerted by a sudden movement, vibration, or other disturbance. If you move slowly and cautiously, the trout will not be likely to associate you with danger, and you can get close to the fish. Because of the trout's narrow feeding lane, you will have to cast accurately. Any sudden movement like the flash from the reflection of the rod, the flick of a fly line, or any other unnatural motion will quickly alert the trout to danger. Most of the trout's predators strike with lightning speed, and the trout is fully equipped to react accordingly.

Planning Before Casting Is Essential

Before casting to a fish or to where you suspect a fish might be holding, have a plan for how you'll hook, fight, and land it. Often, a hooked fish swims toward a nearby structure. Determine the best angle from which to get the necessary leverage to pull the fish away from that structure.

The best position to fight a trout is from across or downstream of it. That way the fish is working against the current and you are pulling the hook into the fish's mouth. The riskiest position is if you hook a fish straight downstream of you. If you do hook a fish downstream of you, get below it to fight and land it, even if that means backing out of the water, getting on dry land or in shallower water, and moving swiftly downstream. It's always easier to pull a fish in if you aren't battling it *and* the current.

Fish Are Attracted to Dead-Drift Streamers

Whether fishing from a boat or wading, most people cast streamers to the bank and retrieve them straight back, though most baitfish do not swim upstream or rapidly across many currents. Not only is this technique unnatural, but according to John Barr, fish on pressured waters get so used to seeing streamers fished this way that they ignore them. These same fish, however, are suckers for a dead-drifted streamer. Fish your streamer like a nymph, throwing in a few twitches now and then to imitate a crippled baitfish drifting the current. Bottom dwellers like sculpins and madtoms immediately head for cover when threatened, so that means you have to get your fly on the bottom, which is nearly impossible with a swung fly and a floating line. Cast far upstream, letting your fly sink as it travels past you, and gather slack with your other hand so that you are ready to strike when a fish takes and the tip of your floating line lurches forward.

Fish Feed Facing the Current; Not Always Upstream

One of the reasons that approaching from downstream of fish is so effective in moving water is that fish feed by facing upstream into the current. By approaching from behind, you significantly reduce the chances of being spotted. But it is important to remember that fish do not always face upstream; they face into the current. Especially in eddies and lazy Susans—large eddies near river banks with swirling, circular currents—fish may appear to be facing downstream, but are actually facing into the current. Pay attention to the direction that the water is moving and adjust your presentation accordingly. Look for foam, debris, or insects on the water to help you track the currents. In still waters or slow sections of river without much current, fish will cruise in all directions. The key to catching these cruisers is to not cast at the rise—that is where they were—but rather to anticipate the direction they are heading and try to put your fly there.

Fish Gather in Undisturbed Waters

Scared fish are hard (if not impossible) to catch. Get to the spot first, and your fishing will be easier. This doesn't mean that you should rush to fish a particularly good pool before your buddy gets his rod rigged up, but if you are fishing behind another angler, especially a careless one, you may never see a fish—they will all have spooked. If you can, fish during the week, fish early and late in the day, and walk a lot—some of the largest fish are at the end of the longest walk.

Another way to be first to the fish is to concentrate on overlooked water. Most anglers focus on the deep water in pools, but there are other holding or feeding lies in a stream that are often passed by. Shallows can provide good fishing, especially in low light; fast pocket water and bouldery runs produce good fishing, and slots and depressions in the runs often go undetected by everyone but locals. Another simple tactic is to cross to the side of the river opposite the road or access trail. Most anglers don't walk far from their cars, and most don't bother crossing to the other side of the river.

Large Rivers Can Be Divided for Easier Handling

Large rivers can seem intimidating at first, but they have all the same features as smaller streams. If you don't know where to start, break the river down into smaller parts. The riffles, inside corners, runs, and pools that you are familiar with on smaller streams are there, they are just bigger. Stalk the shallow water for big fish, especially if there is food available and it is near deep water. Riffle drop-offs and seams indicate prime habitat. Braided sections of large rivers and side channels have great habitat, are easier to wade, and are often too shallow for drift boats to pass through, which means they often go unfished. And remember, just because it is big water doesn't mean that you have to cast 80 feet out into the middle of it. Most of the fish will be along the banks, so make sure you fish that water first.

Slack Line Must Be Managed

Whenever you're fishing upstream, whether with dry flies or nymphs, the line, leader, and fly will begin drifting toward you as soon as they land on the water. Slack occurs in the line between the fly and the rod tip, and if you let this slack accumulate on the water, you'll have to remove it after a fish takes the fly and before you can move the hook to set it. To prevent this, always gather slack as soon as it forms, simply by drawing it in through the guides with your line hand. You can lift your rod to take out some slack, but don't lift it so high that you have no room left to lift it to set the hook if a trout hits.

When fishing downstream, you'll find many times when you want to feed slack into the drift to extend it. If you are casting dry flies over rising trout, feeding slack can be critical for reaching fish sipping just where your fly might start to drag. When you are shot-and-indicator nymphing, the fly might reach strike zone depth, down near the bottom, as it drifts back even with you. By feeding slack to extend the drift downstream, you keep the fly in that zone a lot longer. Wiggle your rod tip back and forth to draw slack out through the guides and lay it in S curves on the water in front of you. Then as it feeds out, it will not cause drag.

Fly Speed Can Be Controlled by Mending the Line

When you cast across currents, the moving water typically produces more leverage against the thicker, heavier running part of the fly line than it does against the lighter, thinner front taper and leader. This causes the back of the line to move faster downstream, forming a downstream belly in the line. Your dry flies will begin to drag, and if you're fishing a nymph rig, the belly will speed the drift of your indicator and lift your fly away from the bottom.

To counteract this type of drag, use an upstream mend to lift the belly off the water and flip it over into an upstream curve. The dry fly or strike indicator will then float without drag until the slack is pushed back out of the line into another downstream belly, at which time you must mend again. On slow water, you can use a downstream mend to catch the current and speed the swing of a wet fly or streamer. Most of the time you'll make small to big upstream mends to slow the drift or swing of all types of flies.

Fly Should Be the Last Thing to Change If You Have a Refusal

Often trout rise to your dry fly and seem to take it, but you miss the strike. You'll think it's because you're too slow setting the hook. More often, a missed strike is caused by the fish refusing your fly, rather than your failure to set the hook. The trout changes its mind at the last second; you see a boil or a splash, but it's not a real take.

When you get refusals, check your leader first. Is it long enough? Is your tippet long and fine enough for the size fly you're fishing? If not, correct it. Next, check your presentation. Are you getting drag you can't see? Is your leader arriving ahead of the fly, so trout see it and turn away? Move to the best casting position, and choose the best cast to avoid drag. The last thing to look at is the fly, which is the first thing most of us want to change. It's almost always best to go a size or two smaller, and a shade or two drabber, when you get refusals to a dry fly and need to change it.

Fast, Broken Water Makes It Easier to Catch Fish

When approaching a stream for the first time, one effective strategy is to focus your efforts on the faster water—the heads of pools, runs, and riffles are prime spots. Look for spots where the surface currents are broken, but avoid water that is rushing so fast that you'll have a hard time getting your fly to the fish. Fish feeding in slow flats are way more difficult to catch than fish in broken water. Currents break up the trout's view of above, provide cover that makes them feel less wary, and mask the noise of your approach; and in fast water, trout need to make a quicker decision than in slow water. In slow water you may only have one shot at a fish, but you can drift your nymph or dry fly through broken water many times. Faster water is also more forgiving of sloppy fly casts, making such areas good places to start.

Microdrag Can Be Beaten by Changing Position

Sometimes it may look like the fly is drifting naturally, but the trout continues to ignore it. Consider the subtle influences of the current pulling against the fly, what Marinaro called "hidden drag." In *The Ring of the Rise* he offers the following advice: "All of us are victims of hidden drag. If you really want to find out the truth about this, you can try the following experiment: Take a small chip of paper or wood as big as a finger-nail, and toss it out into the current. Get below or downstream and make your best cast with the fly as close to the chip as possible. Watch them closely as they move along. If the fly veers away only slightly, merely an inch or two, you have a fatal drag. Don't try it only on a nice smooth, straightforward current; try it in different areas. You will be astounded and perhaps depressed by the result."

It only takes a slight change in current speed to move the leader enough to create microdrag. There are many situations where it is impossible to get a natural drift, no matter what adjustments you make in tackle or presentation. Normally, you can't detect microdrag; you have to anticipate it by changing to a lighter tippet, extending the length of the tippet, or extending the total length of the leader. Changing position is one of the best ways to overcome microdrag, yet it is a tactic seldom used by even the most experienced anglers. Moving to another spot from which to make your cast can often make all the difference.

Predatory Skills Are Important

Knowing what the trout are feeding on, selecting the proper fly to match, and presenting the fly in a natural manner isn't enough to consistently catch selective trout. Like any other predator, a fly fisher must learn as much as possible about how to find, stalk, and capture his or her prey. This was of prime importance when our ancestors relied on hunting, capturing, and killing for survival. Today, many of us are as out of place in the world of nature as a sumo wrestler at a soccer game. The more we can learn about a trout and its behavior in its environment, the better our chances will be to deceive it.

In hunting, woodsmanship is more important than the ability to call game or shoot straight. The best hunters are those who possess a keen knowledge of the game they pursue. It isn't until the game is located and stalked that calling ability or shooting skill comes into play. The same can be said with fly fishing. It won't do any good to be a great caster or to understand how to select the correct fly if you can't locate a trout and stalk it into position. Predatory skills can be the difference between success and failure.

In *Fishing Small Flies*, Ed Engle adds simplifying your gear as part of the secret to becoming a successful hunter of fish: "Reduce everything to the basics. Determine what you need for where you fish, know how to use it, have confidence in it, and leave the rest in the truck. Reducing the stuff will give you the freedom to concentrate on the trout, or more precisely, the prey...Angling at its best is trout stalking and trout hunting. You would do well to think of yourself as a predator. Go light, lay low...follow your instinct...and put as little as you can between the trout and yourself."

Fishermen Cooperate by "Telling Time"

Being able to communicate a fish's location to your partner is a critical skill when sight-fishing—whether on a spring creek or the flats. Using the clock-face method, you can be sure to have a common language to help you communicate a fish's location, which is far more effective than screaming "fish, over there!!!" at the top of your lungs.

The method that works best when fishing from a boat is to tell time when pointing out a fish to your partner. In a boat, the bow is always 12 o'clock, 9 o'clock would be 90 degrees left, and 3 o'clock, 90 degrees right. In addition to telling the time, also call out the distance and direction of travel, such as "coming toward the boat," "going away," or "moving left." While the spotter is calling out directions, the caster should move the rod tip to confirm the direction. The caster should not cast until he or she can also see the fish.

Good Guides Are Good Teachers

One way to learn more quickly is to hire a good, competent guide—not a guide who grabs your line right off and ties on a yarn ball indicator as big as a grapefruit with a couple of beadhead nymphs to drift below. With this terribly effective method, the guide can adjust the boat enough to keep the yarn ball drifting without drag and keep the nymphs at the proper level. He can almost guarantee you catch fish, maybe more than anybody else on the river, but you won't learn much. You need a guide who will work harder, do more, teach more, and help you catch a few fish in the process.

There are three good reasons to hire a guide. The best reason is for instruction and expertise. A guide will help you cast, read the water, choose the right equipment, and teach you anything else relating to the sport. More importantly, with a guide you'll most likely get some hands-on experience hooking, playing, and landing fish. Next, even if you are already an accomplished angler, a guide can help you learn about the area. Finding fish is one of the biggest challenges in fly fishing.

Explain to your guide what you want to accomplish. Sure, you want to catch fish. If that's all you care about, and you don't care how you do it, he'll probably start you off with a yarn ball and some nymphs, and you'll catch fish. If you want more, you'll need to let the guide know. Most guides are skilled anglers and excellent instructors, and they welcome the opportunity to teach the techniques of fly fishing, even if it means their clients catch fewer trout.

Rough Water Could Cause a Wet Fall

If the water you intend to wade has any depth and potential danger to it, be sure to carry a wading staff. Also cinch a belt around your waist to prevent your waders from filling entirely if you should take a plunge. Tie the staff to the belt with a couple of feet of cord. When wading boisterous water, always keep one foot and the staff planted, and do not move the trailing foot until the leading foot has found a firm seat on the bottom. If the water is pushy, use the staff on the upstream side; lean into the current and onto the staff at the same time. If you should ever get knocked loose from your moorings and fail to regain your footing, don't panic—you're just in for a wet ride. Despite what many people think, if your waders fill with water, you will not sink. Just tuck your chin to your chest and elevate your legs, and use your hands to paddle to shore. Above all else, remain calm.

Trips Require Preparation for the Worst

Though no one likes to fish with a naysayer, think of the worst-case scenarios when you are packing. Lefty Kreh offers the following sage advice based on over sixty years of traveling around the world: "It is going to be hotter than they say, colder than they say, wetter than they say, and someone will forget the lunch."

Even on local trips, carry a change of clothes and socks in a water-resistant or waterproof bag in case you fall in. You can leave it in the truck if you are fishing nearby, but if you're going out in a boat, take it with you. Keep your cell phone, camera, wallet, and any other valuables or electronics in a dry bag. A Ziploc baggie provides inexpensive insurance against rain or a quick spill. Always keep a few energy bars stored in your vest. Always tell someone where you are going. On long-distance trips, consider buying trip insurance and renting a satellite phone, which is cheap insurance if your guide has motor trouble out on a flat somewhere in the Bahamas.

Reading Water and Finding Fish

Stream Banks Can Tell You How to Fish

Steep banks usually drop off into relatively deep water, and they often have vegetation growing down to the river's edge. Trout or bass could be anywhere in water that runs between steep banks, but the odds are good that many of them will live in the luxury housing along the edges. If you want to fish on the surface between hatches, look for steep shorelines, ideally those with trees, brush, or grass. In a warmwater stream, slap a popper, a grasshopper pattern, or a big cricket against the bank. In trout water, try a beetle, ant, cricket, or, in late summer, a hopper. During the afternoon, you're more likely to find fish willing to rise along the shaded bank.

Gently sloping banks let a river spread out during high water. At its normal level, the stream might have long, wide stretches of exposed gravel and sand along its edges. Generally, the water next to these gravel beaches is shallow. At night, trout or smallmouth might come to the edge of the shallow water to hunt stone fly nymphs, hellgrammites, or minnows. During the day, though, shallow water flanked by low, gradually sloping banks holds few fish. Here the topography steers you toward the center rather than the edges. Since the water in the middle of the stream receives little or no shade for much of the day, the fish living out there probably congregate in the deepest spots from midmorning until early evening. Throw a weighted nymph or streamer at them.

Easy Wading May Mean Poor Fishing

There seems to be a correlation between the quality of the fishing and the beating that a riverbed inflicts on your feet and ankles. The places that hold the most fish food and game fish are also those that make your feet most sore. The more surface area and variety a riverbed has, the more life it can support. A mix of coarse gravel, pebbles, assorted rocks, and large stones has millions of nooks and crannies where insect larvae, crayfish, and small fish hide and feed. Because it's uneven, such a bottom creates many pockets of slow or slack water where trout, bass, or panfish can hold.

Bedrock or long stretches of smooth, uniform bottom composed of sand and a little gravel support relatively few invertebrates that fish can catch (nymphs that burrow into a sandy bottom are rarely available to trout) and give the fish nowhere to hide from the current. A flat, sandy bottom makes for easy wading, but it probably won't make for good fishing. Move quickly through such areas, but keep an eye peeled for isolated features—a fallen tree, a clump of rocks, a patch of weeds—that might hold a fish or two.

Slippery streams with uneven bottoms covered with algae on which felt-soled boots slip and slide often support a respectable quantity and variety of insects, and some of them produce pretty good hatches. Streams that aren't as slippery can lack the nutrients that let algae thrive. And they lack the bugs.

Foam Indicates a Fish Food Bank

If you find yourself at a loss for where to drift your fly on the water, identify those currents that concentrate foam and other debris, and fish your fly through them. These are the prime conveyor belts of the trout stream, and when a hatch is on, trout hang under these food superhighways waiting for the bugs to come to them. Even when there is no hatch, trout are accustomed to hanging out near these spots, waiting for an easy meal to come their way. For instance, when the current reaches a rock that juts out from the bank, it moves all the food into a tight drift lane around the rock. The rock also buffers the current, making the narrow drift lane just below and to the side of the rock an excellent source of food. Just in front of the rock is also a great spot because the concentration of insects slows down before sliding around the rock. Back eddies and slower water along the bank also become prime spots for trout to lazily slurp the hundreds of insects that gather there during and after a hatch.

Fish Avoid the Sun

Trout and bass have a fixed iris that doesn't dilate to control the amount of light that enters the eye. They don't, therefore, particularly care for bright sunlight. They like areas that provide shade when there aren't enough insects on the water to move them out. In hot weather, midday is usually the slowest time on a trout stream, but you can frequently still find rising trout in shaded areas under trees and other bank structures. Shaded areas are prime feeding locations, and the dominant fish will usually run other fish out of these locations. When it is sunny out, work the shady side of the river; and look for trees and bridges that throw shadows on the water. Avoid flat water baking in the sun, and focus on riffles and the middle of the deepest pools in the middle of a hot day.

Large Browns Are Active at Night

Major hatches of large insects such as green and brown drakes or *Hexagenia* bring up large fish, but usually under the cover of darkness. In the east, aquatic moths and large stone flies (*Pteronarcys* species—even larger than western salmonflies) often emerge or lay eggs at night. Most anglers never see them, but the fish know they are there. Night fishing for trout, especially brown trout, is best when the daytime water temperatures reach their highest. Though night fishing is not for everyone, it offers the brave of heart a chance to catch the largest fish of the year.

Practice casting during the day with your eyes closed to prepare for casting and managing line in the dark. Explore your night fishing spots during the day. Bring a headlamp, but use it sparingly. Not only does the light spook fish, but it throws off your night vision, and after you turn it off, your pupils will have to readjust. To help you see, you can fish larger-than-usual patterns with big white wings. (Change your fly to your night rig before it gets too dark to see.) Larger flies and less light mean heavier tippets. You'll also need to have heavier tippets to fight the fish quickly and from your position—you won't have the luxury of chasing a strong fish downstream. The safest thing to do is to stand your ground and hope your tippet holds.

The Most Comfortable Part of the Day Is Best for Fishing

Because fish are cold-blooded, they can't change the temperature of their environment, but they can move around to find the most comfortable spots. Move to the same spots, and you'll catch more fish. In the spring and fall, when the water is cooler than it is in midsummer, the best fishing usually doesn't start until at least a few hours after sunrise. There's not much point in getting up before dawn to fish in a river full of early spring snowmelt or one chilled by a week of frosty October nights. If you're on the river early in the morning, work the slower, calmer water with a nymph or midge larva, and keep the fly close to the bottom. Cold, sluggish fish don't like to fight strong currents, and they won't expend much energy to take a fly. As the sun warms the stream, the fish spread out, and more of the river comes alive. By lunchtime, you can start to catch fish in riffles, runs, and the downstream ends of pools. In the summer, fish early and late when it is cooler.

Small Streams Should Be Thoroughly Covered

Creeks can vary from mountain torrents to foothill feeders to lowland meanders. Headwaters tend to be steep with successions of plunges, deep pools, and runs along and above protruding and submerged boulders. Trout hold where obstructions—boulders, logs, rootwads—break the current and where depth protects them from predators. You'll find most trout close enough to the main current to dash into it and take whatever food trots past them.

The key to catching trout on creeks is moving and covering lots of water. Brush on both sides of the creek might constrict your rod movement and get in the way of your back cast, so you may have to walk upstream in the water, casting your fly under tree limbs and other snarls. Strip your gear to the essentials and carry it in a belt, shoulder, or chest pack, or a short and light vest. Even better, pare your gear to what fits in your shirt pockets. Condense your flies to a single box of attractor dries, nymphs, and soft-hackled wet flies, such as the Royal Wulff, Elk Hair Caddis, and Beadhead Hare's Ear. Tuck a Windbreaker, shirt, or rain jacket into a pocket or tie it to your fishing bag, and carry a water bottle on your belt.

Change Is a Good Thing

People new to trout fishing make a common mistake: they get rooted to one spot doing one thing, and fail to change even when they fail to catch trout. Here's a logical sequence of change to consider whenever the fishing gets poor.

Fly pattern. Change to a fly in the same style you're already using—dry, wet, streamer, or nymph—but a smaller one, larger one, darker one, or lighter one.

Presentation. Try changing the direction from which you approach a lie and cast to it. Read the water carefully for conflicting currents. Then take the best position to present the type of fly you're fishing.

Type of fly. If you're not catching fish on dries, switch to wets or nymphs. Often when they appear to be feeding on the surface, trout are actually taking something just beneath it.

Depth. Try changing the depth at which you fish your fly. If it is a wet or streamer, switch to a sinking-tip line. If it's a nymph, add a split shot or two on the leader, or slip the strike indicator up a foot or two.

Water fished. If you've fished awhile in one spot and haven't hooked anything lately, no matter what else you've changed, then move on. You've probably worn out the place and put the fish off their feed.

Water type. Switch from riffles to pools or from runs to bank water. Find the water type where the trout are holding, then concentrate on it.

Stream fished. If the stream you're on is not producing, hasn't for a long time, and doesn't promise to soon, then try going somewhere else. Fishing might be hot in the next watershed over.

Water Properties Determine Prime Fishing Locations

It has often been said that 10 percent of the fishermen catch 90 percent of the fish. That is extreme, but some fly fishermen get a lot more action than others. The critical skill that elevates them is not the fancy rods that they fish, nor their casting ability. It is primarily their ability to read water and find fish. They fish water that contains trout. They spend little time fishing water that doesn't.

Reading water is merely a matter of noticing where a stream meets the basic needs of trout: protection from predators, shelter from strong currents, and food. Locate places where these three things are available, and you'll likely find trout. The best way to learn to read water is to go out and catch fish, and then to remember what the water looked like where you caught them. Not a bad assignment.

Catching and Releasing

Slow Risers Require Slow Strikes

When a trout takes a fly from the surface, it also inhales the water and air. With the fly in place, it closes its mouth and exhales water and air through its gills. If you strike the fish before the trout closes its mouth, the fly will most likely pull free. The most common reason we miss hookups is that we strike too quickly. In slow water or for big fish, New Zealanders say, "God save the queen," and then strike.

Trout rise slowly when the current is slow and smooth. They have plenty of time to inspect the fly before it drifts through their window of vision. It sometimes takes nerves of steel to keep from hauling back on the rod and line when the nose of a 4-pound trout pushes through the surface film and sucks in the fly. If the fish is downstream, you must wait longer to tighten into the fish because the line pressure is pulling the fly back out of the trout's mouth. The chance of a hookup is greatly reduced if its mouth is still open when you strike. Wait until the trout closes its mouth before you tighten the line.

Upstream Fish Require Quick Strikes

Since trout always face into the current, you should time the strike differently if you are below the fish than if the fish is below you. When you are downstream from the trout, you will be pulling the fly back against the trout's mouth when you strike. You can strike more quickly and still hook the fish, even if its mouth isn't completely closed over the hook. If you wait too long to set the hook, the fish can feel the fly or leader in the corner of its mouth and reject it before you set the hook. In fast water, fish have less time to inspect the fly, and often take it quickly, rushing up through the currents. If you wait too long to strike, you'll miss the fish.

Strong Tippets Land Heavy Fish

The longer you fight a fish, the more you stress and tire it. It may seem impressive to land a large trout on a superfine tippet, but you should use the strongest tippet possible and land your fish quickly. George Harvey advocates using a tippet heavy enough to land a fighting trout in a reasonable amount of time. When he fishes with a big fly, like a Green Drake, he uses a 3X or 4X tippet, and even with small flies he rarely uses anything smaller than 6X because he feels it isn't fair to the fish.

A simple formula you can use to determine the correct tippet size to use in relation to the size of your fly is called the rule of three. Take the size of the fly you intend to use and divide it by three. If the fly is a size 16, the correct tippet size is 5X. With a size 18 you should use 6X. You shouldn't need to use 7X until you start using flies that are size 22 or smaller. When streamer fishing use 0X because the fish doesn't see the leader. Heavy leader allows you to land the fish quickly, cast the flies easier, and pull your streamers out of the bushes without breaking the tippet.

Disorienting the Fish Will Help Land It Faster

Some anglers let the fish fight them rather than the other way around. You can land a big trout in a surprisingly short time if you can keep disorienting it. Use the rod to fight the trout; always apply pressure constant and opposite from the direction the trout is moving. If you keep a good bend in the rod, it will give you a cushion if the fish bolts unexpectedly. You can usually disorient a big trout and land it quickly without tiring it completely. A fish swimming straight into the current is holding its ground, but if you can bend its head right or left, you force it to work against the current, tiring it faster. If possible, try to pull at right angles to the fish's head, and move so that you are downstream of the fish.

Trout Should Be Netted Headfirst

You can land and release many fish without a net by simply using forceps or pliers to unhook your fly from their mouths while they are still in the water. When people try to land a strong fish with a light tippet, however, they tend to overplay the fish, potentially doing more harm than good. With a net, you can land a fish quickly.

Don't try to chase the fish down with the net. Instead, keep the net in the water and bring the trout to the net headfirst. Don't sweep with the net until the trout's head is inside. If the trout senses movement or feels the net, it will panic and bolt. Take the fish from the net as soon as possible to avoid further injury. Older cotton-mesh nets are not as good for the fish as the newer rubber-mesh ones or the ones with soft-mesh bags. Once the fish is in the net, keep him under the water while you remove the hook. Barbless hooks come out easily, limit undue handling of the fish, and are easier to remove from your clothes or skin.

Cameras Are Useful for Capturing a Catch

Nowadays you don't have to put your fish on a stringer to prove you caught a big one. Digital cameras are not only compact enough to fit in your vest pocket, but several water-resistant models are available, which are perfect for fishing and other outdoor activities. Before taking a picture, make sure you have your camera ready to go so that you only have to keep the fish out of the water for a few seconds (no longer than you can comfortably hold your own breath!). The pros advise that you leave the fly in the mouth of a big fish so that you can reel it in again if it flops from your grasp, and you can keep the fish from squirming simply by relaxing your grip and not squeezing it. If you are fishing alone, do not drag the fish onto the bank or on the rocks to take the picture. Not only does it harm the fish, it makes for a horrible picture. When you are by yourself, you can take better pictures of fish by leaving them in the water.

Fish Must Be Quickly Revived

After you remove the hook, immediately return the fish to the water. A good rule of thumb is to never hold the fish out of the water longer than you can hold your breath. Hold it facing into the current, and make sure the fish is working its gills. Release the fish when you feel it has regained enough strength to hold in the current under its own power. Don't leave until the fish swims away. If the fish holds in the same position, give it a few minutes, and then touch its tail with your rod tip. If that doesn't cause the fish to swim away, wait a few minutes and repeat the procedure.

Make sure that the water where you are reviving the fish is not silty and that the current is not too swift. One effective way to increase the amount of oxygen in the water (and revive the fish quickly) is to vigorously splash the water in front of the fish with one hand while you hold it steady with the other. The increased oxygen rushing through the fish's gills helps it recover faster.

A Hook Will Dislodge or Dissolve If Left in a Fish

It's better to leave a deeply embedded hook in a fish's mouth and cut the line than to rip the hook out. Over time, the hook will dissolve or work free, especially if it is barbless. Though there is no existing scientific research on the topic, fish have been observed surviving with hooks in various stages of decay in their bodies.

Many variables determine how fast the hook will dissolve, and if the fish will survive at all. These include hook location (throat, stomach, mouth, etc.), hook size, fish size, temperature (most reactions occur faster at higher temperatures, so a hook would probably dissolve faster in the summer than in the winter). A hook in the mouth might hamper feeding behavior, but only temporarily.

A hook in the gill, however, will almost always prove fatal because it interrupts the respiratory process before it gets a chance to dissolve. Hooks in the stomach will nearly always dissolve, and the fish will live, if internal organs have not received life-threatening damage from the hook (such as during a fight between fish and angler). Fisheries biologists estimate that it would take roughly two to three weeks for an average hook to be dissolved by the average fish.

Wild Trout Are Worth Fighting For

Catching and releasing takes on a different perspective when fishing for wild trout. Few streams in the world can sustain a healthy population of wild trout with much fishing pressure. Releasing fish because we know and understand that they can survive to be caught again is both a good and selfish reason. Wild trout are an intricate part of a vast ecosystem. When you consider that many different birds and animals depend on them for survival, from the ospreys to the bears, it makes sense to protect them.

Hatchery trout usually do not have the instincts to survive in a wild environment. Catchable-size trout that are poured into streams usually don't live long, whether they get caught or not. If streams are overharvested, or their habitat becomes degraded and cannot support wild trout, part of the ecosystem dies with them. Wild trout are not only better game than their hatchery counterparts, but they fight harder, live longer, grow larger, and are more beautiful. Bald eagles, ospreys, river otters, and many other predators add to the fishing experience, and their survival depends on a healthy wild trout population. To watch an osprey dive with a mighty splash and rise from the water with a trout in its talons can be the highlight of an entire day of fishing. Wild trout are precious, and they should be protected.

The Fish and Their Senses

Brookies Aren't Actually Trout

The brook trout, *Salvelinus fontinalis*, is the native trout of the east. Until the late 1800s it was the only trout in the settled parts of the North American continent. It is technically a char, closely related to the Arctic char, Dolly Varden, and lake trout. The brookie is dark green on the back and dorsal fin, with vermiculations that look like lines in a wormwood maze. The sides have numerous yellowish spots, with fewer red spots that are surrounded by blue halos. The tail is only slightly forked, hence the common name "squaretail." The native range of the brook trout extends from the Arctic Circle south to Appalachian headwater streams in Georgia. The inland range reaches streams in Manitoba and the Great Lakes states of Michigan and Wisconsin.

Brookies need cold, clear water, and do not survive in waters that reach temperatures above 75 degrees. They are extremely susceptible to trouble caused by logging, farming, and pollution. In most of their original habitat in the United States, brook trout are now relegated to tiny headwater streams and forested mountain lakes and ponds. The typical fish in such waters is small, but is as pretty as the tiny waters from which it arises. As its preferred habitat has dwindled, the brook trout has been displaced by hardier rainbow and brown trout.

Perhaps Joe Brooks best summed up the nature of the brookie when he wrote, "They zip up from their shelter beside or under a rock, hit, and if you don't hook them, turn and dash back, all in a second, a fleeting flash of wild trout."

Rainbows Are Fast-Water Fish

Rainbows prefer cold, tumbling streams, and are more apt to be caught in riffles and runs than in still pools. They are extremely adaptable, though, accepting habitat conditions that would distress or kill a brookie or cutthroat. The rainbow was originally classified as *Salmo irideus* in honor of its coloring—dark back, silver sides, and liberal dashing of small spots on the sides, tail, and back. A prominent red band runs along the lateral line (can be faint on some fish) and their gill covers are often blush-colored. That classification was changed to *Salmo gairdneri* in honor of the naturalist who first collected and described the species, Meredith Gairdner. In 1988 its name was changed again, to *Oncorhynchus mykiss*, a reflection of origins that are closer to those of the Pacific salmon than they are to those of the Atlantic salmon and brown trout.

The sea-run form of the rainbow is the steelhead. The original range of the rainbow extends from the Aleutian Island chain to northern Mexico, and along the Kamchatka Peninsula in Russia. The rainbow is a transplant in the Rocky Mountain states of Montana, Wyoming, and Colorado, states deservedly famous for rainbow fishing. Before humans and dams and pollution arrived, steelhead ran upstream and spawned in most clean, cold streams with access to the Pacific Ocean. Their range extended far inland into Idaho, where steelhead swam hundreds of miles to spawn in the Clearwater and Salmon rivers, tributaries to the Snake River that flows into the Columbia River. Some steelhead still make the trip despite all of the dams.

The Brown Is the Newest Trout in North American Waters

The history of fly fishing is closely intertwined with the brown trout, *Salmo trutta*. The origins of the first sophistications in tackle, tactics, and fly patterns, most of which occurred in Britain, can be traced to the desire to please the demanding brown trout. But the brown is the newest trout in North American waters. Brown trout first arrived in America in 1883 as a shipment of eggs from Germany. There was a subsequent infusion of eggs from Scotland, which explains the old thinking that the brown was actually two species: the German brown and the Loch Leven brown. They are the same species from two sources. A typical stream brown runs 12 to 16 inches long, has bronze to yellowish brown coloration, with numerous black spots on its sides, tail, and back, and fewer but larger red spots also on its sides.

Browns were established in many eastern rivers of the United States before the turn of the century. In the next few decades they became the dominant fish in most heavily fished eastern waters. Many anglers at the time deplored their presence, blaming the decline of native brook trout on them. But this was sour grapes: the fragile brookie was killed off or driven into marginal headwaters by man's meddling, not by brown trout. The hardier brown was able to supplant the brookie because it was able to withstand the pollution, silting, and warming of waters that killed brookies.

Early American tactics had been worked out on the easily caught brookies, but they didn't work on the difficult import. The brown trout is, perversely, considered the perfect fly-rod fish because of its reluctance to take flies. It feeds on all of the natural foods imitated by artificial flies, but it is highly selective, creating challenges in imitation, tackle refinement, and presentation skills. Brown trout nudged American fly fishermen toward the same refinements of tackle, tactics, and fly patterns that this fish had encouraged in Britain, and for the same reason—to catch brown trout more consistently.

Trout Aren't That Smart

Fishing literature is rife with references to trout so smart they have their PhDs and allusions to "crafty" browns. The truth is, trout are not highly intelligent, but lower on the IQ scale than bass, carp, and goldfish, among others. Bass at least have enough brains to know that a large frog makes a better meal than a water beetle, but trout will often key on a specific insect while ignoring all other food sources. It isn't intelligent to sip tiny mayflies and ignore a big fat moth if you have the chance to eat it. Keen senses and elaborate instincts, not intelligence, keep the trout alive and healthy. These characteristics also make it a worthy opponent.

On heavily fished waters, a trout that has been caught and released will often continue to feed while anglers make dozens of casts over it. It will be difficult, however, to catch that trout on the same fly as before. The fish, which took a fly that was drifting unnaturally in the current, will likely associate a dragging fly with danger in the future. More importantly, as a trout matures it learns to concentrate on the positive. Natural insects drift on the surface without movement. The trout eventually learns to associate its food with this positive trait. It will ignore a dragging fly simply because it doesn't associate the fly with food. In effect, the trout doesn't even see the fly if it isn't drifting exactly the way the trout's natural food is drifting.

Trout Are Individuals

Don't think you've solved the mystery because you've caught one trout. Trout have individual personalities and behavior traits. One trout may prefer one kind of insect while other trout are feeding on different insects. Common sense dictates that the trout will feed on the largest, most numerous insects, but you can't assume anything in trout fishing. It is not uncommon for trout to show a preference for a smaller insect even if there are good numbers of bigger flies on the water, what are sometimes called, in fly fishing lingo, "compound hatches." When stalking trout, use binoculars to watch your quarry closely, and try to determine exactly what the fish is feeding on before selecting a fly.

Fish Can't Hear You Talking

Fish cannot hear our voices, but sound waves traveling five times faster in the water than through the atmosphere can either attract or frighten fish. A trout can detect the difference between the sound of a grasshopper falling into the water and an angler clumsily wading through the water. Trout living together in smooth flowing currents can display interesting schooling behavior when frightened by a sudden underwater sound or vibration. The panic of a single fish will instantly transmit to the others, sending them scurrying for cover.

Like other fish, trout use a concentration of nerve endings along their sides, called the lateral line, to detect vibration. The lateral line will detect vibrations from crunching gravel caused by walking carelessly along the bank even though the sound waves don't enter the water. Because of these sensitive lateral lines, flies that push water are effective, especially at night or in cloudy water where trout can't rely as heavily on sight.

Odors on the Fly May Matter

Trout have an acute sense of smell, which they use to find a mate during the spawning season, detect minute differences in the chemistry of the water to find their way back to the stream from which they were born, or even sense danger. Water passes continuously across the olfactory organs within a trout's nostrils as the fish swims, leaving it to discern the complex chemical composition of the aquatic environment.

While we have a good biological understanding of the trout's sense of smell, we still do not fully understand how a trout perceives odors and discriminates among them. Anglers disagree whether scent left on a fly pattern from an angler's hands or the chemicals from dry-fly floatant cause a trout to reject the fly. (Some fly pastes are scented with chemicals that are said to attract trout.) To be safe though, some New Zealand guides don't wade upstream of wary browns, and many good guides everywhere will rub mud on their hands before fishing to get rid of cigarette, sunscreen, or bug repellent odors. Because sunscreens, bug repellent, and gasoline can also ruin your fly lines, you should take care of these things before you go fishing and then thoroughly wash your hands. Even though a trout can detect the odor of your hand, the fly materials, and the floatant, it probably doesn't rely on smell until after it has decided by visual inspection to accept or reject the fly.

Fish Don't Have Hands

One of angling's great pleasures is to relax on the stream bank and watch a trout feed. Even the most selective trout rises to take a small twig, a leaf, or a weed seed, and then promptly spits it back out again. It notices the object, takes it into its mouth, and then smells, tastes, and feels it to make a final determination. Trout use their strong sense of touch and feel to confirm whether what they have taken is food.

Because fish take flies so quickly and spit them out, it is important to fish a tight line and watch the fish if you can for signs of a take. It is often too late if you wait for your strike indicator to twitch. Better instead to watch for the white mouth of a trout taking the fly or a sudden flash, and then set the hook. Some anglers say that the Hare's Ear and other shaggy flies are so effective because the fibers catch on a fish's teeth, sort of like Velcro, making it difficult for them to spit out quickly.

Color Is the Least Important Attribute of the Fly

Trout do not regard color as highly as other factors such as size and shape. Aquatic insects of the same species vary widely in color. Take, for example, the western pale morning dun mayfly. One book describes it as pale yellow, another light chartreuse, another pale yellow/olive, and another grayish yellow. The male and female of most mayfly species are different shades, the female being usually lighter in color. One of the best-known mayflies of the East and Midwest is the Hendrickson. The male is dark rusty tan and the female is light pinkish tan. Individuals of this species also vary in tints of color. Although there are thousands of different species of aquatic insects, most fall into a few common color categories: dark, grayish insects in early and late season, and lighter shades of yellow insects in the summer (with exceptions).

Trout see color differently than humans. Trout have less control over the amount of light that enters their eyes because their irises do not dilate. Bright sunlight washes out the natural color of an insect, and low light neutralizes its color. The natural color of an insect is most important during optimum light conditions— during morning and early evening hours when trout get a more accurate color reading of the fly. But even then, size, profile, and where the fly is riding in the water are more important than color.

Trout Try to Spend the Least Amount of Energy Possible

When feeding, trout try to expend the least amount of energy possible. The streamlined anatomy of a trout and its fin structure enable it to hold in the current without swimming against it, much like a hawk can sail on and on in the thermals without ever moving its wings. In *A Modern Dry Fly Code*, Vince Marinaro addressed the economy a trout must use to survive. "During the whole of his life he is forced to practice extreme economy of movement, never exerting himself unduly. His frugality in this respect makes even human indolence seem like sheer extravagance . . . Ordinarily, a trout can be played to complete exhaustion in a matter of minutes with the gentlest resistance, even when he is in the best of condition." The reason trout feed selectively on midges but ignore a random dun is that they can expend less energy filter feeding the small, abundant insects rather than coming up through the currents to take a larger bug. Look for places where trout can feed easily, such as currents that bring the food to the fish, and try to identify the most abundant food items—not necessarily those that are the easiest for you to see.

Big Fish Usually Don't Make Splashy Rises

Don't be fooled by the rise a fish makes. Experienced anglers know that a large fish can make a small rise and that splashy rises tend to come from smaller fish that haven't yet learned how to conserve their energy or from fish that are chasing after fast-moving insects such as caddis flies, dragonflies, and damselflies. Big trout have the uncanny ability to sip or suck the naturals from the surface, making little disturbance on the surface of the water. To spot the soft rise of a big trout requires patience. You may need to spend a good amount of time watching the surface of the water. It helps immensely if you know the water. Big trout usually like to hang out in the same places.

The Biggest Trout Hold the Best Feeding Spots

Trout feed by facing into the current and letting the current carry their food to them. The feeding station that the trout selects offers the best opportunity to intercept drifting insects. The most dominant trout, which are usually the largest, occupy the best feeding stations in any given pool. If the dominant trout is taken out of a pool, the trout next in line to the dominant trout will usually take over the prime feeding location.

It takes a keen eye to spot primary feeding locations. The flat surface may look the same all over at first glance, but underwater vegetation, subsurface depressions, rocks, undercuts, logs, and bank structure all create enough change in surface currents to concentrate food and provide resting areas for trout. As long as the structure of the stream doesn't change, these feeding spots, or prime lies, will remain the same year after year.

Food and Flies

The Right Mayfly Pattern Catches the Desired Fish

Mayflies have three important stages. The first stage, the nymph, lives on bottom stones or swims and crawls about in vegetation. At rare times trout might take them selectively down there; most of the time they feed on them at random, along with lots of other things. A generic nymph such as a small Hare's Ear or Pheasant Tail imitates the real thing closely enough.

The second stage, the dun, emerges at the surface. It is the most important stage of the mayfly. Duns resemble little sailboats, and come off in fleets, so trout key on them, and often refuse anything else. Because mayfly duns hatch out in open water, they are vulnerable to trout. Match them with Comparaduns, traditional Catskill dressings, or Hairwing Duns in the appropriate size and color.

The last stage, the spinner, lays its eggs and falls spent to the water, usually at evening. When clouds of spinners descend, trout key on them, and you have to match them. You can do it with simple dries that have hackle splayed out to both sides, or you can fish a sparse wet fly just under the surface.

Caddis Flies Have Three Growth Stages

Caddis flies also have three important stages. The larval stage lives on bottom stones or crawls about in rooted vegetation. Most build cases and are relatively safe from trout. But many stream types—the green rock worms—build no case. These live in riffles, and trout often feed on them. Bright flies such as the Green Caddis Larva should be tumbled right on the bottom in fast water. Caddis pupae squeeze out of the larval case and dash to the top for emergence. This brief transitional stage is very difficult to observe. When you see caddises dancing in the air over a stream but cannot catch trout on dry flies, suspect pupae, and fish soft-hackled wets on the swing.

Adult caddises are erratic fliers, difficult for trout to capture, so they often hit them with quick, splashy rises. Try the Elk Hair Caddis or Deer Hair Caddis. Many adult caddises deposit their eggs by swimming under the water. If you see lots of caddises dancing in the air at evening, but again cannot take trout with dries, try a winged wet the same size and color as the adults in the air.

Caddis Larvae Are More Important Than Adults

Caddis flies are one of the most common and widespread of all aquatic insects. There are approximately 1,400 species of caddis flies, outnumbering the total amount of mayfly and stone fly species combined. They live in both flowing and still waters. Caddises are also the most tolerant of polluted water and higher water temperatures, making them critical insects in marginal or seasonal trout streams.

Every fly fisher has seen the little mothlike adults flying around streams and near bankside vegetation. Fishermen always talk about hatches, because that is what produces the most glamorous and fun fishing. The reality is that most of a trout's caddis fly diet is the larva, and during a hatch, trout feed on more pupae than actual adults.

Stone Flies Are Either Nymphs or Adults

Stone flies have only two important stages. The nymphs live on the bottom, usually in water that is charged with lots of oxygen: rapids, riffles, and fast runs. They vary in size from tiny 16 up to giant 4. Imitate the largest with weighted nymphs such as the Kaufmann's Black Stone and Kaufmann's Golden Stone in sizes 4 to 8 tumbled right on the bottom.

Adult stone flies scramble about in streamside vegetation, and make short awkward flights out over the water. They often fall in, and often get taken by trout. Dry flies such as the Sofa Pillow and Stimulator work well in sizes 4 through 10. Fish them dead-drift, usually as near to the banks as you can get them.

Yellow Sallies are important summer stone flies that frequently hatch on headwater streams, and small black stone flies can be important early-season insects on many trout streams. Often, your caddis imitations can do double duty for some of these smaller stones (for dries), and to imitate the nymphs you can use largish Hare's Ear Nymphs.

Midges Are Attractive in Large Numbers

Midges are generally tiny, sizes 16 through 22. Some species in the northern range of trout habitat are as large as size 10. But most are small, and are attractive to trout only when they emerge in great numbers, which they do often. Midges are especially important in spring, fall, and even winter when other insect hatches do not occur.

Midges have two important life stages. The first is the pupa, which ascends slowly to the surface, then hesitates at the surface film before breaking through for emergence into the adult stage. Imitate the pupae with sizes 14 to 22 nymphs in standard black, or in olive and red color variations. Fish these on a long, fine leader and floating line, up near the surface in smooth water.

The second stage, the adult, is best imitated with patterns such as the Adams or Parachute Adams in the very smallest sizes. A Griffith's Gnat, which is no more than a peacock herl body with grizzly hackle wound over it the length of the hook shank, floats flush in the surface film and represents the adult trying to escape the pupal shuck. Such simple dressings often work alarmingly well during midge hatches.

Terrestrials Represent a Variety of Insects

Trout don't pass up any insects that fall to the water from grass, brush, or trees alongside the stream. Such luckless creatures make up a large part of the trout diet at certain times of the year. Grasshoppers get blown into the water on hot and windy summer afternoons. They are important on streams that meander through fields and meadows. Imitate them with patterns such as Joe's Hopper and the Letort Hopper in 8 to 12. Tiny ants get into lots of trouble on trout streams. They're difficult to observe on the water without the aid of an aquarium net. Most pattern books will list dressings for 18 to 22 Black Ants and Cinnamon Ants. Beetles fall to the stream in a variety of sizes and colors—ranging from plain black to the iridescent green of the common Japanese beetle. Those that you want to match will normally be small. Deer hair patterns such as the Crowe Beetle and Deer Hair Beetle in 16 to 20 work great, but they are not as durable as foam imitations. Bright green inchworms rappel down to streams on their fine silk threads. Imitate them with bright chenille wound on a size 10 to 14 hook, and fish them wet beneath overhanging branches.

Dry Flies Can Be Combined Two at a Time

Many anglers have caught on to the effectiveness of Hopper Dropper rigs (a dry fly and a nymph), but you can also fish two dry flies at the same time. Fishing two dun patterns at the same time is useful if you want to increase your chances that fish will see your fly, or you want to fish different dun patterns to figure out which pattern they prefer. You can fish a fly that is hard to see—because of poor light or because the fly is small—behind an easy-to-see indicator pattern.

In riffle water, Hoppers or Stimulators work well as indicator flies, but when fishing in flatter water for crafty fish you want to use a less obtrusive, more imitative indicator fly. There are a number of good choices for visible dry flies that blend in with the hatch, such as various-sized Parachute Adams tied with high-visibility parachute posts made from brightly colored poly yarn.

Tough Trout Are Attracted to Sunken Spinners

Mayflies eventually transform into spinners. Once spinners mate, the females fly over the water's surface where they deposit eggs that eventually sink to the bottom. Some species, most notably those of the genus *Baetis*, dive or swim under the surface and deposit their eggs on the bottom. After mating and laying their eggs, the spinners die. Many end up on the water, a phenomenon anglers call a spinner fall.

Most spinner imitations are designed to float on the surface of the water, but more and more anglers are discovering that spinners fished under the surface can be more effective, and provide good fishing for several hours after the fish have stopped feeding on the floating insects. Trout love to stack up downstream of a riffle that shelves off and gorge on drowned spinners. You can tie your sparse spinners on heavy wire hooks to help them sink or use a small split shot.

Insect Bubbles Create Sparkling Meals

Most aquatic insects create or trap bubbles of gas at some time in their lives. They use these bubbles for respiration, buoyancy, and as an aid for escaping the subadult form. Whatever reason these insects use bubbles, all reveal themselves to trout as dazzling quicksilver images that appear to glow with an inner light. Bubble-encased bugs are extremely visible underwater, and trout often swim right past other food items to snare a glittering insect. Many times trout will key in on and feed only on sparkling insects. When the time is right, bubbles trigger takes.

The easiest way to apply bubbles is to treat your nymph like a dry fly. Shake it vigorously in fly desiccant powder such as Shimizaki Shake or Frog's Fanny. Even better is to actually scrub the desiccant into the nymph fibers.

Adams Was Originally a Caddis Imitation

Len Halladay, from Mayfield, Michigan, named this venerable generalist pattern after Ohio attorney, Charles Adams. The fly is thought to have been designed to imitate the caddises and stone flies common to Halladay's favorite trout waters, including the Boardman River, where the fly was reputedly first tested in 1922. Nowadays, most anglers pluck this pattern from their box to match mayflies.

The fly was traditionally tied with webby grizzly hackle wings, a mixed brown and grizzly hackle and tail, and a muskrat-fur body. The Adams's subdued colors match many of the early- and late-season mayflies, and many think the mix of brown and grizzly hackle are so effective because they suggest movement. The Adams is an excellent choice for a searching fly when visibility is not essential—the drab colors can be hard to see. Tied in smaller sizes (18–22) it can represent midges, and in larger sizes it suggests a host of drab-colored early- and late-season mayflies. Though it originated in Michigan, many people incorrectly call this a Catskill pattern, one variation of which is called the Delaware Adams. The Parachute Adams is another popular variation of this fly.

Elk Hair Caddis Works Skittered and Sunk

Al Troth, originally from Pennsylvania, first tested this hairwing caddis imitation on Loyalsock Creek in the 1950s. "It was supposed to be a floater and it floated all right, but not for long," Troth, seventy-seven, said in an interview in the *Montana Standard* published May 10, 2007. "I gave it a tug and it went under, and I hooked a 20-inch brown." Troth moved to Dillon, Montana, in the early 1970s.

This simple and elegant fly pattern remains effective today. Tied in different sizes and a few different colors such as green, tan, brown, and black, this fly imitates most of the major caddis and small stone fly species that you are likely to encounter. Anglers most often fish this fly dead-drift, but one particularly effective technique is to cast quartering downstream and lift the tip of the rod, allowing the fly to skitter across the currents on its stiff hackles. The hackled version is ideal for riffles and other broken currents; if you want to fish the pattern on more placid waters, trim the hackles flush on the bottom or tie it without hackle. And, if fishing it dead-drift or skittering it across the surface doesn't produce results, do like Al did and tug it under.

Royal Patterns Work Wonders

Lee Wulff created the Wulff series of flies in the winter of 1929–30, a series that includes Royal Wulff, Gray Wulff, White Wulff, and others. Of all of these effective flies, the Royal Wulff, a beefed-up version of the Royal Coachman, is the most popular. Lee Wulff writes in *The Art of the Trout Fly* that he invented the Wulffs "in rebellion against the typical British-type dry flies" and opted for a chunkier, more appealing looking morsel than the sparse patterns prevalent on trout streams at the time.

Who knows what this fly imitates, but it floats well, anglers and fish can see it easily, and perhaps because it imitates nothing in particular, it elicits reaction strikes from fish. It is a great searching fly and makes an excellent buoyant pattern off of which to hang a small nymph when fishing a dry and dropper rig. The prominent white wings are highly visible. This fly is best in larger sizes up to about 16; in smaller sizes it is hard to tie. It is a deadly fly for Atlantic salmon and steelhead when tied in larger sizes.

Stimulator Is an All-Purpose Stone Fly and Caddis Imitation

The Stimulator was invented by Oregon angler Randall Kaufmann to imitate an adult stone fly, and it was undoubtedly inspired by the effectiveness of Pat Barnes's Improved Sofa Pillow, Troth's Elk Hair Caddis, and other flies. Perhaps the Stimi has become a legendary pattern because it has many components of successful patterns built into it. This hairwing stone fly and caddis imitation tied in different color combinations works well on tumbling currents anywhere and is an excellent indicator pattern in a dry and dropper rig. The original pattern was tied with a yellow body and an orange head, but green and orange, all orange, or black and orange are popular variations. Tied in yellow it imitates golden stones, in orange stone flies, and in green (in smaller sizes) little lime sallies that hatch on small headwater streams. Kaufmann's original tie has a splayed hair wing to suggest movement of the fluttering wings of the natural stone fly when it is riding the currents, but commercially tied versions of this pattern are a little tamer in appearance.

Woolly Bugger Imitates Everything

Credit for the Woolly Bugger's invention goes to Pennsylvanian Russ Blessing, though it was probably inspired, at least in part, by the old British Woolly Worm. Perhaps no other fly pattern has been tweaked and modified more than the Woolly Bugger, so much so that Gary Soucie's book *Woolly Wisdom* includes over four hundred patterns spawned by this simple, but deadly, fly.

People have a hard time classifying it as a streamer or a nymph—and it can be both, depending on how it is tied and fished. Tied heavily weighted and bounced along the bottom with

short strips, it imitates a crayfish; fished dead-drift, a hellgram-
mite or stone fly; and twitched, an escaping baitfish. In still
waters, you can fish this pattern with a slow hand-twist retrieve
to imitate a damselfly (tie it sparse) or dragonfly (tie it chunkier).

False Casts Can Help Dry Flies

Minimal false casting is the sign of efficiency. A good caster
doesn't make eight false casts for each presentation; he'll pick up
30 feet of line and leader and develop enough speed with a single
false-cast cycle to drop the fly 50 feet away. With a nymph or
streamer, that's great. Learn to make your subsurface deliveries
with as few false casts as possible. With a dry fly, however, an
extra false cast is not wasted effort because it helps blow-dry the
fly. You can often get another half-dozen drifts out of a soggy fly
simply by adding an extra false cast to each delivery. When the
current or a submerged leader drags a dry fly beneath the surface, try not to let it stay submerged too long. Get it up in the air
and use a false cast or two to dry it off, but watch where you
make false casts. Line flashing back and forth over a trout will
spook the fish. Water spraying off the line and leader can do the
same thing. Keep your extra false casts short and off to the side of
the target, and then lengthen the line and change direction to hit
the target.

Behavioral Drift Is an Overlooked Hatch

Even in moderate weather, fish move to different areas at different times of the day. Many anglers assume that insect activity
refers only to hatches, but aquatic insects also engage in less obvi-
ous activities. One of these is something that entomologists call

drift. At dawn and dusk, larvae move around more than they do during the middle of the day. Some of them deliberately let go of the streambed and drift downstream for varying distances; others lose their footing and become captives of the current for a little while. What all this activity means to fish is that the larvae of mayflies, caddis flies, stone flies, and midges become more visible and available early in the morning and again in the evening. In part, drift explains why we often enjoy the best fishing early and late in the day: There's more going on underwater, even if we don't see it.

The challenge is figuring out which nymph or larva pattern to cast during these drift periods. Only local knowledge can provide an exact answer, because the mix of insects varies from river to river, but we can make some educated guesses. Entomologists tell us that nearly every healthy trout stream contains a sizable (if mostly invisible) population of the larvae of midges, caddis flies, and small olive mayflies. That suggests certain fly patterns: midge larvae, caddis larvae, and little olive or Pheasant Tail nymphs can be effective.

Distinctive Patterns Sometimes Work Best

Trout get aquatic insects in very large doses. The season's population of a species emerges at a certain time each day for a short period, resulting in a tremendous concentration of food. When insects blanket the water, matching the hatch perfectly while making a faultless presentation often isn't enough. How can you get the trout to pick your fly if it is only taking one mayfly and letting the next twenty drift past? Somehow, you must draw the trout's attention to your pattern. You might have to show the fish something different so that it notices it. If, when a trout starts to poke his nose up, there are ten naturals in the area, you might get better results if your fly looks different from the naturals. Not only is the fly easier for you to see, it is easier for the trout to see. Small terrestrials like beetles or ants or small attractors like a Parachute Adams or a Royal Wulff are good choices. A slight, well-timed twitch to the fly just as it is entering the trout's window can focus its attention to your pattern and away from the multitude of insects. If you wait until it is well within the trout's window of vision, it will most likely draw too much attention and put the fish down.

Confidence Patterns Provide a Fallback Plan

Develop a small list of flies with which you've had success and that give you confidence. Keep them handy in a single fly box. They need not imitate particular insects, but should resemble in a broad way the natural foods that trout eat. The best dries resemble lots of different foods. The Adams, Elk Hair Caddis, Stimulator, and Humpy are examples of standby dry flies.

Each season, go through your boxes and weed out any duds or patterns that you didn't need. This will streamline the selection of flies that you carry on stream, and you'll spend more time fishing your flies rather than poring over a multitude of choices. While trout do often demand a precise imitation, you'll often have success by fishing an appropriately sized pattern designed realistically with the same general profile and color of the naturals.

Dry Flies Should Be Kept Floating

If your dry fly fails to float, it won't fetch many fish. It's not that fish won't take a sunken dry, it is just that if your dry fly is under the surface, you'll have a hard time fishing it well. To keep it floating, use a handkerchief to dry the fly often, and then re-dress it with floatant. Watch an expert sometime. He constantly dresses his fly between pools, or between fish. He watches the water while he does it. This keeps his fly floating primly, but also causes him to slow down and assess the situation, so he is more apt to present the right fly in the right way, and therefore catch the right fish.

For CDC (Cul de Canard) feathers, use Dry Magic, amadou, or Frog's Fanny. Do not use gel floatants because they mat the fibers and cause the fly to sink. Rejuvenate flies that have been slimed by fish or waterlogged with a desiccant such as Shimizaki. When your fly fails to float well—even after using these treatments—retire it and let it dry.

Bubbles Indicate Trout Feeding at the Surface

If there is a small bubble in the rise, the trout has definitely taken something from the surface. When it expels the water and air it inhaled with the insect, the bubble is the result. If there is no bubble, it still may have taken something from the surface but just sucked it in without taking air in the process. If you see a bulge or other disturbance that doesn't break the surface, the trout probably took a nymph. When trout are feeding on nymphs at the surface, you should fish the nymph very much like a dry fly. The nymph should be tied on a light wire, dry-fly hook. Apply dry-fly floatant to the tippet except for the last inch or so above the nymph. This will keep the nymph suspended just under the surface film. Cast above the working trout so the nymph will drift through its feeding lane. Strike whenever you see the trout move.

Size Matters

The difference in hook size is greater between size 20 and 22 than between 10 and 12. The smaller the fly, the more size matters. Many times, changing to one size smaller makes all the difference. You've chosen the wrong size when your fly stands out from the dozens of small mayflies on the water because it is slightly larger than the naturals. Before you choose a fly, capture one of the naturals and notice its size. It can be tempting to try to get away with a fly pattern that is too large, and many anglers are reluctant to change to a fly they can't easily see.

Proportion is also more critical the smaller the fly. Remember, a trout chooses the size of the entire fly, not the hook size. Small flies are frequently overdressed, making them appear a size larger than they really are. This can be a real handicap. I like to use as large a hook as possible on small flies. Sometimes you can trick the trout by underdressing a small fly. A size 22 hook tied with size 24 proportions will look like a size 24 fly to the trout. You can also tie a smaller pattern on a short-shank hook. A 1X short hook means the body size of a size 20 fly will be the same proportion as the body on a size 22 hook. Tails also make a fly look larger—try trimming or cutting off the tails if a fish refuses your large pattern and you don't have a smaller one.

Position of the Fly Is Important

The correct size, color, and shape of a fly will not matter much with selective trout if the fly is not in the right position in, on, or under the surface. A thin, firm layer on the surface of the water called the meniscus helps keep insects floating on the surface or holds them just under the surface. Think of the meniscus as three levels: on the surface, in the surface, and under the surface.

Emerging insects are often suspended just under the surface film as they try to escape their aquatic shells and penetrate the meniscus. Many insects become trapped within the surface film, where they are extremely vulnerable to feeding fish. Adult insects rest on the surface film, pumping fluids into their wings and drying them in preparation for flight.

You can fish a dry fly on the surface, or you can modify it in the field to fish in the film or even just under the meniscus. You can fish a nymph deep, but also grease the leader or even the fly to get it to float. Don't be afraid to fish your fly in different parts of the film depending on where the fish are feeding.

Flowers Provide Clues to Insect Hatches

Mayfly hatches coincide with bloom periods of common trees and flowers. Learn to recognize these patterns and record them in a journal. Hatch-matcher Charles Meck first planted the seed of this idea in *Great Rivers, Great Hatches*. Canadian Bob Scammell contributed to the body of knowledge of western hatches with *The Phenological Fly*.

For example, in Pennsylvania, blooming forsythia or wild ginger indicate that anglers should be on the lookout for Hendricksons; blooming mountain laurel signifies slate drake time; and wild rhododendron, tricos. According to Scammell, sighting brown-eyed Susans mean *Hexagenia* are emerging, and at the first signs of clematis blooms, he starts looking for western March brown in his neck of the woods, Alberta. Watch wild specimens because microhabitats near houses and in suburban gardens can expedite bloom times.

Equipment

Knots Should Be Tested Early

After you cinch a knot tight, give it a few steady pulls to make sure it holds. It's much better to know right then and there that your knot is weak than after you hook your only nice fish of the day. Before cinching any knot tight, lubricate it with water, saliva, or a lubricant such as lip balm.

Before you get to the stream, practice your knots at home with old pieces of fly line so you can tie them smoothly when fish are rising all around you. You can also test one knot against the other by taking a 12-inch piece of tippet and tying one end to a hook with one knot, and tying the other end to another hook with another knot. Pull both hooks with pliers to see which knot is stronger. Wear eye protection when you do this.

Household Soap Can Be Used to Clean Fly Lines

If your fly-line tip sinks, chances are your line is dirty. (Another cause of a sinking line tip is a leader butt that may be too heavy.) Other symptoms of a line in need of a good scrubbing are a visibly dirty line, a line that doesn't shoot well, or a line that makes a rattling, scratchy sound as you shoot it through the guides.

Not all fly lines are made the same. Some have additives applied to their surfaces that help them float and remain supple, and some have internal lubricants. The best way to clean all fly lines is with soap, not detergent. If the product doesn't say "soap" on the label (such as Ivory hand soap or Woolite), don't chance it.

Strip the line from the reel in large coils (that land on top of each other) into a bucket, your tub, or a sink of hot water with a drop or two of soap. Do not put in too much soap or you will have trouble getting your line free of the soap, which leaves a film on your line if you don't get it off completely. Soak the line for about fifteen minutes to loosen grit and grime. Scrub the line with a damp cloth or sponge. Drain the soapy water and fill the sink with clean water. Rinse the sponge or cloth repeatedly so that you remove all excess soap and dirt.

Neutral-Colored Fly Lines Work Best

Many anglers think that a bright fly line cast over a trout is more likely to send it scampering for cover than a drab one. A dark or drab fly line will blend into the surroundings, especially on smaller streams with a lot of green vegetation along the banks, but a bright line is easier for you to see and track, which helps your accuracy and helps you keep your false casts out of the trout's view. With a dark line you'll sacrifice the advantage of being able to keep track of the line, but you will probably spook fewer trout. More important than line color, however, is good casting technique that never puts the line over the trout. Cast sidearm to keep the line and rod low, and false cast to the side of the trout.

Several fly-line manufacturers produce neutral colored lines, including olive, which show up well against the water, but also blend in with the surroundings. You should consider the water you plan to fish before you make a decision on the best color for a fly line. Remember, the trout will be viewing the line from below. A line that blends in with the dark vegetation along the bank of a smaller stream might show much more contrast against a light sky on a large, open tailwater. Clear-tip fly lines offer the advantage of basically extending your leader by 15 or more feet, and many consider them essential for spooky bonefish or trout—but they are also harder to see.

Good Sunglasses Are Essential Gear

Polarized sunglasses cut glare on the surface of the water, allowing you to see trout holding under the surface. Don't try to cut corners with polarized glasses. Look for high-quality glass or polycarbonate lenses that not only cut glare but also protect your eyes from ultraviolet rays. Lenses come in a variety of colors and shades. The darker the lens, the less light it allows through, so choose light lenses for low light conditions, amber or brown for general fishing, and dark gray or brown for saltwater fishing on the flats or out on lakes. Side shields cut down on the amount of light that enters the eyes from the sides, making it easier to spot fish. Use a strap to keep the glasses around your neck when you aren't wearing them. When you take an extended fishing trip, always pack a pair of backup glasses.

Tackle Must Match the Fly and Fish

Tackle is usually selected backward. We wobble a rod and like it so we buy it. Only then do we buy the lines and leaders and flies. Tackle selection should start at exactly the other end, with the fly to be fished. What a fish eats dictates the tackle that should be selected to fish for it. Tarpon eat baitfish the size of trout; you could not cast tarpon flies well with trout tackle. Trout eat insects; you would not get feathery presentations by casting trout flies with tarpon tackle.

Food size dictates fly size, and fly size dictates leader size. The leader must be tapered to transfer the unrolling power of the line down to the fly. It must be stiff enough to lay the fly out at the end of the cast, yet light enough to allow the fly a natural drift once it is on or in the water. The taper of the leader and the size of the fly dictate the line weight that will deliver the best presentation with the least effort. Large flies, especially weighted flies, boss a light line around; their hooks end up in your earlobes. Tiny flies fished with heavy lines go whap! to the water, and frighten wary trout. When everything is in balance the line loops out; the leader arcs over at the end of it; and the fly, leader, and line all land straight and lightly on the water right where you aim them.

Casting Rods Are Different from Fishing Rods

Graphite came in with the Space Age and swept fiberglass aside in the late 1970s and early 1980s. It is a light but very strong material. Graphite comes as a cloth, which is cut and wound on a mandrel, like fiberglass. The result is a hollow rod that is thinner than glass, and much lighter than either glass or cane. Rods built of graphite are a quantum leap over both glass and bamboo in terms of the power-to-weight formula.

New generations of graphite appear at intervals, each one stronger than the one before it, and the current trend is for fast-action rods that create high line speed (basically, tips that don't wobble back and forth when you stop them, which creates larger loops). Higher line speed is an advantage in distance casting, but it is not always an advantage in trout fishing. Greater line speed magnifies mistakes and makes them happen in a hurry. Since most casts in fishing conditions contain a litany of little errors—some of which are installed intentionally to achieve a specific purpose in the cast—most of us are better off, at least at first, with trout rods that forgive them. The refinement of graphite has led to racks of rods that are light and sweet, that cast smoothly, and that present flies with rhythm and grace. A person setting out to select one must merely remember that the goal is to catch trout close at hand, not cast across the horizon.

Few Fly Rods Are Broken by Fish

Proper care of a fly rod is mostly a matter of keeping it away from slamming car and screen doors and out from underfoot. Very few fly rods are broken on fish. Another easy way to break a rod is to walk along with it out in front of you like a lance. If you fail to mind it, the rod will poke a tree, or droop until its tip jams into the ground. It's best to carry a rod with the tip behind you most of the time, especially if you are threading through trees and brush. If you carry it in front of you, get in the habit of holding it with the little finger of your carrying hand over the handle. This points the tip high, and prevents it from drooping.

When joining a rod, line up the guides and seat the sections firmly, with your hands held close to the ferrule. When taking it apart, pull in a direct line, with your hands slightly away from the ferrules. If the rod is stubborn, don't pull too hard or your hands might slip and damage the snake guides. Enlist some help, but don't get into a tug-of-war—one guy on the butt section and the other on the tip. Each of you should put one hand on each side of the ferrule, then pull with increasing force until the rod comes apart, which it will with surprising ease.

"X" Ratings Measure Leader Diameters

In the old days of silkworm gut leaders, this natural material was extruded through fine holes to elongate it into leader sections that were then tied together. A 5X leader section was extruded five times, thus was much finer than a 3X section, extruded only three times. Modern leaders are still rated by the "X" system, but it now refers to the leader diameter in thousandths of an inch. A 5X leader is .006 inch, a 3X is .008 inch. It makes more sense to refer to the diameter than it does to the "X" rating of a leader. Both are printed on leader spools. Not all leaders of the same diameter are the same strength, which is why fly leaders are referred to by diameter rather than pound test. Manufacturers vary a lot. Because leader brands vary in strength and in relative stiffness or limpness, you should avoid tying two different brands together.

Simplified Leaders Minimize Materials

Buy a few basic knotless leaders in two lengths, for example $7^1/2$ and 10 feet, and always carry them in your vest. Make them one size stouter than you would normally use, for example 2X or 3X if you usually fish 4X or 5X for size 12 to 16 flies. Then buy and carry spools of the most commonly used tippets, such as 4X, 5X, and 6X, in the same brand material. When you get to the lake or stream and choose a fly to tie on, add the appropriate length and diameter tippet to the basic leader for that fly and situation. This simplified process prepares you to meet nearly any fly fishing situation with a minimum of materials to carry.

Lefty Kreh and others tie loop knots onto the ends of the leaders and then loops on their tippet sections, and attach the tippet to the leader with loop-to-loop connections. Done in this manner, you'll be able to fish that leader for a long time, since each time you tie a surgeon's or blood knot to connect your tippet it shortens your leader.

For most dry, wet, nymph, and streamer fishing, a leader the length of your rod or a bit longer will be about perfect—between $8^1/2$ and 10 feet. When fishing small dry flies over rising trout on smooth water, use a 10- to 14-foot-long leader, with the fine tippet 2 to 4 feet of that length. Use tippets about 2 feet long for most fishing, but 3 to 4 feet if you're fishing over fussy trout. If the leader gets cut back to 15 inches or so as you change flies during the day, then take time to tie on a new tippet that is the original length.

Different Situations Require Different Line Weights

Line weight designations are only manufacturers' recommendations for each rod. Fly lines are matched to rods based on 30 feet of line in the air. Most rods can handle several line weights, depending on your skill level and the amount of line you are casting. Sometimes it pays to over-line or under-line your rod depending on circumstances. The most common reason to fish a line weight higher than what your rod is rated for is to make short casts on small streams, where casts are often less than the 30 feet for which the rod is rated. The most common reasons to under-line are to make more delicate presentations with your rod or to cast for distance. If you typically carry and cast more than 35 to 40 feet of line, then you might find it easier to do so if you under-line your rod. For every 10 to 15 feet added to the 30 in the air, you add another line weight to the load—a 5-weight line becomes the equivalent of a 6-weight when 40 feet of line is aerialized, a 7-weight with 60 to 65 feet in the air, and so on.

Kinks Should Be Removed from Leaders Before Fishing

The easiest thing to do to improve distance, accuracy, and hook sets, and reduce the amount of tangles in your line, is to stretch your line and leader before fishing. This step only takes a minute, yet most anglers don't bother doing it.

Store-bought leader straighteners (generally two rubber pads covered with fabric or leather) are unnecessary and can generate too much heat, which can weaken monofilament nylon. To stretch your leader, stroke it with your hands, applying as much pressure as you can. The heat from the friction will straighten the leader. Stroke the butt repeatedly until it is straight. While stretching the leader, check for wind knots and abrasions, which can weaken your leader. Check your line and knots frequently for damage or abrasion. If there's any doubt, replace the tippet. Even small nicks weaken your tippet.

For accurate casting you also need to stretch your fly line. You can pull on the line with both of your hands to stretch it or wrap it around a fence post or tree and pull on both ends. If you are in a boat with limited space, the best way to get the kinks out of your line is to strip off 6 feet, step in the middle of the line, and pull up on both ends with your hands. Do this for all the line that you anticipate casting.

Fly Reels Do More Than Just Hold Line

You often read that fly reels aren't important, and that they just hold the line. That is partially true. Unlike spinning reels that have an integral role in the casting and retrieving of line, most of the line's manipulation in fly fishing is done with your hands, including playing many small fish.

The best thing to do with larger fish, however, is to get them to the reel as quickly as possible, either reeling in all of your slack line, or letting the fish pull out all of your slack. If you are fishing fine tippets, you want a reel with a smooth disc drag that does not pay out the line in starts and stops, which could break off a 6X tippet. You also want a reel with a drag that doesn't create backlashes every time you strip off the line.

Casting

The Line Must Be Moving Before You Cast

Lefty Kreh's Casting Principle 1 states that you have to get the end of the fly line moving before you can make a back or forward cast. To see this in action, place a garden hose on the lawn and put a wave in it to resemble a potential sag in your back cast. Pick up one end of the garden hose and begin walking while looking at the other end of the hose. You won't move the far end of the hose until you remove the large curve. Likewise, to get the end of the fly line moving, you need to remove all slack from the line. If the line is not completely straight in front of you, you waste effort getting the line straight before you can start moving the end. This same principle applies to plug and spin casting—you cannot cast a stationary plug with slack in the line. Before making a back cast, quietly lift all of the line from the surface of the water. Ripping a fly line from the water can alert or frighten nearby fish and waste casting energy.

It's Not the Power, It's the Stop

Kreh's Casting Principle 2 states that once the line is moving, the only way to load the rod is to move the casting hand at an ever-increasing speed and then bring it to a quick stop. A good casting stroke begins slowly, but smoothly and decisively, gradually accelerating to an abrupt stop. The sudden stop at the end of the cast is often called a power stroke, but applying "power" can spoil the cast. Instead, at the end of the acceleration, briefly move the rod hand even faster and then stop it abruptly. The stop is critical in delivering the total energy of the cast toward the target. Any immediate follow-through of the rod, after the stop, opens the loop and reduces line speed.

The faster you accelerate the rod hand in the first portion of the casting stroke and the faster the hand speeds up and stops, the more energy the rod stores and the faster the line travels. The stiffer the rod, the more potential energy it can store, and the farther back the rod bends, the more energy stored in the rod for the moment you stop it. As you move the rod forward, if you accelerate a short distance (even with a spinning plug or lure), you only bend the top of the rod and therefore only store energy in the tip, which is the weakest part of the rod. Have somebody hold the end of the fly line in his thumb and first finger, as you just bend the tip of the rod; he can hold the line easily. If you walk forward a few more feet and bend the rod more deeply, you can pull the line right out of his hands.

A Mousetrap Can Be Used to Practice Casting Weighted Flies

Kreh's Casting Principle 3 states that the line goes in the direction the rod tip speeds up and stops. Once you throw a ball toward a target, you cannot change its direction of travel. Once the rod straightens on the stop, you cannot change the direction of the cast—you could throw the rod away and the line will still go in the direction of the stop. Anything that you do to the rod after you stop doesn't affect the direction of the loop. Lower the rod and you will lower the line, but the fly still goes toward the target.

When casting weighted flies, such as beadhead nymphs or bonefish patterns, many tend to tilt the rod slightly so the weighted fly won't hit them on the forward cast. Right-handed casters tilt the rod to the right. But on the stop the tip will flex slightly to the left, and since the line goes in the direction the tip stops, the weighted fly curves left as it falls to the water, spoiling accuracy.

A good exercise to practice casting weighted flies accurately is to use a mousetrap. Set the trap and place it 30 to 40 feet away from you. Cast a weighted fly (with the hook clipped off) at the trap and try to trigger it. Tip: The most accurate way to cast weighted flies is to come straight over the top on your forward cast.

The Rod Should Be Moved Farther Back on Long Casts

Kreh's Casting Principle 4 states that the longer the distance the rod travels, the less effort is required to make the cast. A short back or forward rod stroke only bends the tip of the rod. As the rod moves through a longer stroke, the fly line continues to build line speed and increase the bend of the rod. A caster with a shorter stroke must exert more effort to obtain the same line speed and load in the rod.

A fly rod is a flexible lever, and the farther back you bring it, the more it helps you make a cast. When making a short cast, you do not need to move the rod back far. When you have to cast farther, throw heavy or wind-resistant flies, defeat the wind, or make a number of special casts (even when trout fishing small streams), bring the rod farther back and forward. This longer stroke also gives you more time to pull out slack in the line. The longer the rod travels forward, the more slack can be removed.

A Good Grip Is Required

Gripping the fly rod is like gripping a baseball bat, golf club, or tennis racquet. If you are up at the plate and about to hit a ball, gripping the bat hard the entire time will compromise your swing, you won't hit the ball very well, and your hands will hurt at the end of the day. Good hitters grip the bat just before they make contact with the ball. You don't grip your golf club hard the entire time you swing for a long drive, you grip it just before you hit the ball. When serving in tennis, you grip the racquet just as the ball makes contact with it, not through the entire swing. You hold the bat, club, or racquet just enough to control it through the stroke. Through the fly casting stroke, only grip the rod hard just before you speed up and stop. Blisters or red hands at the end of a practice session or day on the water are signs that you are gripping the rod too hard, which is common for beginners.

Lefty Kreh advises anglers that keeping their thumbs behind the target on top of the cork grip is the grip that allows you to make the best stop with the rod. If the thumbnail travels back from the target and toward the target, the rod tip travels straight. Many small-stream anglers put their pointer fingers on top of the cork, but that pointer finger is not nearly as strong as the thumb so you can't accelerate or stop the rod as easily, especially with heavier rods.

Casting Should Be Practiced
Before Arriving at the Stream

The best time to practice casting is when you are not fishing. While distance casting and double hauls are good to practice, your fishing will benefit much more from practicing how to control loop size and accuracy. Use household objects to practice your stroke. To improve loop size and accuracy you can stretch two pieces of rope, garden hose, or bright fly line (use an old line) 4 to 6 feet apart, and stand so that the rod tip is about 1 foot inside the nearest rope and ready for a back cast. Try to cast so that your back and forward casts land between each section to improve your loop and refine your stroke. As soon as you can cast between lines that are 4 to 6 feet apart, reduce the distance.

Another good exercise for loop size and accuracy is to mount a hula hoop on a post (or have a friend hold it) and practice casting through it to improve loop size and accuracy. Begin at 30 feet and move out to 60 feet as you are consistently able to cast a loop through the hoop. Hint: It's easier to cast through the hoop with a sidearm cast than it is with an overhead cast. Whenever you practice, clip the hook off your fly, and wear sunglasses to protect your eyes.

Appropriate Footwork Is Important

Footwork is an overlooked aspect of fly casting and fishing. Whether wading a fast flowing stream or standing on the bow of a rocking boat, the wider your stance, the more stable you are, and the better able you are to allow your body to help you make the cast.

Most good casters advocate casting with your right foot back because that gives you the widest range of motion with your body, but there are a few terrific distance casters that advocate putting the right foot forward because that stance allows them to stop faster on the forward cast. All adopt a relatively wide, shoulder-length stance for balance and range of movement. Most right-handed casters do better if they adopt a wide stance with their right foot behind them—for distance casts or when fishing heavy rods. With a wider stance, you can bring your arm back easier. When making a back cast, shift your weight to your rear foot; on the forward cast, shift your weight to your front foot.

Lines Are Unrolled, Not Cast

The basic casting stroke is the same with fly, surf, plug, or spinning rods. The only difference is that you unroll the line toward the target when you are casting a fly. And the word "casting" can be misleading. Lures and bait are cast on spinning or plug tackle, but fly line unrolls to the target. When fly fishers think of casting the line, they tend to overpower the rod hand, which creates shock waves and other problems. Think of unrolling the line, and your presentations become smoother.

If you are not shooting line, any line that is straight out from the rod tip is not moving, which is similar to tracks on a tank. The tracks on the bottom of the tank are stationary and the tracks on the front end are moving and pulling the tank along. The closer the forward end of the line (the leader end) to the stationary part of the line, the tighter the loop. The most efficient cast has high speed and a small loop that unrolls directly away from and then directly toward the target. Large vertical or side loops distribute the cast's energy around a curve and not to the target, and are more air-resistant than small ones.

Cracking the Whip Means
Slow Down the Stroke

If you begin your forward cast too soon, you might crack the whip. Not only does this sudden unrolling of the line make a loud noise—like a whip—it can cause the line's outer coating to separate, forming cracks in the front of your fly line. If you see these cracks, don't blame the line company, improve your technique.

Lefty Kreh teaches one effective way to prevent coming forward too early. If he has a student who comes forward too soon or too late after the back cast, he asks him, "Where do you live?" He then has him say the following expression as soon as the rod hand begins to move on the back cast: "Ohio [substitute any state name here] is a good place to be from." If he is coming forward too soon, he tells the student he is coming forward when he says, "Ohio is a good place." If he is coming forward too late, he tells the student he is really saying, "Ohio is a good place to be from—from—from." This works exceptionally well to about a 40-foot back cast.

Headwinds Require Smarter Tactics

Many anglers try to make long casts when the wind is blowing in their faces, but unless you are a top-notch caster, you are better off shortening your leader, getting closer to your target, and working less line. Often the chop on the water caused by the wind will allow you to get much closer to the fish without spooking it. Other tactics for dealing with the wind include fishing sinking lines, casting more aerodynamic or heavier flies that are less wind-resistant, or casting tight loops, but most experienced anglers recommend reeling in some line. In fact, whenever you start to run into casting problems—loading the rod fails, your loops are shot, your haul goes to pieces—reel in line, take a few deep breaths, and slow down to get back into the groove of things.

A Good Back Cast Makes a Good Forward Cast

Without a good back cast, you'll never have a good forward cast. So even though anglers most often present the fly on their forward cast, anglers like Lefty Kreh and Ed Jaworowski make the case that it is critical to refine your back cast in order to become a great caster. Looking at your back cast is not bad form, as some anglers suggest, but the best thing that you can do, especially when you are casting a long line—you can't fix it unless you know it's broken. You can also film your back cast by setting up a video camera on a tripod and analyzing your mistakes later.

To make a good back cast, begin the cast with your rod tip as low to the water as possible without any slack in your line; aim your back cast opposite (180 degrees) your target; and keep a firm wrist. Begin your forward cast while the back cast is still unrolling, not after it has straightened completely. The rod will load instantly, increasing the bend in the rod and making it easier to cast; and you will finish with the rod tip and line going forward, rather than down.

Information in this book was excerpted from *Spring Creeks*, by Mike Lawson (Stackpole Books, 2005); *Barr Flies*, by John Barr (Stackpole Books, 2007); *1001 Fly Fishing Tips*, by J. Nichols (Headwater Books, 2008); *Fly Fish Better*, by Art Scheck (Stackpole Books, 2005); *Fishing Small Flies*, by Ed Engle (Stackpole Books, 2005); *Trout Rigs and Methods*, by Dave Hughes (Stackpole Books, 2007); *Fly Fishing Basics*, by Dave Hughes (Stackpole Books, 1994); *Tackle and Techniques for Taking Trout*, by Dave Hughes (Stackpole Books, 1990); *Fish Food: A Fly Fisher's Guide to Bugs and Bait*, by Ralph Cutter (Stackpole Books, 2005); and *Casting with Lefty Kreh*, by Lefty Kreh (Stackpole Books, 2008).

Also *in the*
100 Things t**o** Know *Series*

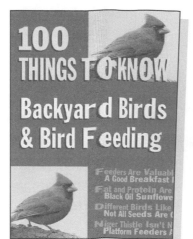